Hot Tips for the Reluctant Housewife

BY SHELAGH NUGENT

ILLUSTRATED BY KOURTNEY HARPER

Nightingale Press

an imprint of Wimbledon Publishing Company

LONDON

Copyright © 2001
Illustrations © 2001 WPC

First published in Great Britain
by Wimbledon Publishing Co. Ltd
London P.O. Box 9779 SW19 7ZG
All rights reserved

ISBN: 1903222 27 3

Produced in Great Britain
Printed and bound in Hungary

The author is a woman of a certain age who is currently working as a freelance writer, as well as being the editor of three small press magazines. She's had more jobs than most people have had hot dinners, for the simple reason that when the novelty wears off, she moves on.

Thank God the novelty of writing hasn't worn off yet because she can't think of any place she wants to move on to - and besides, she's getting past it.

At the risk of being accused of sexism, I'll be referring to housewives of the female gender throughout this book. House-husbands, in my experience, tend not to suffer pangs of guilt, neither do they worry about matching towels in the bathroom, clothes pegged out to dry in the wrong order, general untidiness or a few germs. If you happen to be a house-husband obsessed with dried flowers, china figurines and the dusting of skirting boards, I suggest you seek counselling.

Housewives fall into three categories:

a) Those who take a pride in the Home Beautiful and are quite happy to spend hours on end polishing, hoovering, cleaning and re-arranging ornaments.

b) The guilt-ridden career woman who feels she should be doing more but is always tired and fed up with the pointless drudge of it all.

c) The slob - who doesn't give a damn anyway.

If you fall into category (a) or (c), you don't need this book. For the (b) types, the following is a guide on how to get away with it. If you follow my advice, you can set yourself free. Your friends will envy your creativity, your free time, your popularity, your individuality and will be swooning at your feet in admiration. They'll walk into your home and be amazed at the prevailing atmosphere of happiness and calm. It's true they'll have to shift a pile of magazines onto the floor before they can sit down, you may have to rummage in the dishwasher to find a clean mug for their coffee, if you offer a biscuit, it'll be straight from the tin ... but does it matter? Does it really matter at all?

Think of all the things you could be doing with the time you save not doing housework. Sit down and make a list. No ... never mind the dishes for now, this list is far more important. Get your priorities right.

This is my list of things I'd rather be doing: writing; reading; messing about in the garden; going for long walks; gossiping with friends; slurping fine wine; slurping any old wine; enjoying leisurely dinners; having long conversations with my lover; bonking ... need I go on?

It's not so hard - honestly. Take my word for it - it's all to do with common sense, arranging your priorities and state of mind.

DUST

Whatever you do with dust, it keeps coming back. The more you polish, the more it builds up. You spend ages with the spray can, moving things off shelves, squirting, rubbing, replacing the clutter - what happens? Next day it's back.

That wonderful gay gentleman, Quentin Crisp, never dusted his flat. He reckoned that after three years it didn't get any worse. Mind you, he could probably be placed in the 'slob' category and didn't care.

I don't like dust, it irritates me. You can suck it up with one of those little mini-vacs - or you can set in on 'blow' and waft it around from time to time. It doesn't seem to make a lot of difference what you do.

It seems to me you have two choices:

a) leave every surface un-cluttered so the dusting can be done with one swift swipe of the duster;

b) jam-pack all your shelves with books which don't show the muck. This is my chosen solution. And aren't books a lot more interesting than ornaments? You can read a page or two during the time you've saved not dusting.

DRIED FLOWER ARRANGEMENTS

Dust harbourers and naff to boot. Everybody has them. Do you want to be the same as the mob? Give them away. If you want a bit of colour, you can't go wrong with a bunch of dandelions in a jam jar. As soon as they wilt, chuck them on the compost heap and consign the jar to the bottle bank (you don't even need to wash it!). Start again with a Marmite jar full of daisies. Your friends will be swift to copy - but you'll be ahead of the game, because as soon as they're on to bluebells in coffee jars, you'll be up to assorted weeds in baked bean cans. You get my drift? Be a trend setter. This is all part of the devious plot - dare to be different and your friends will think it's cool not to conform. Your house-cred is being established. While you're chilling out with a glass of wine, they'll be scouring the verges looking for something original. You're not bothered because you've already put a few of next-door's hedge trimmings into a milk bottle.

LACY
SCATTER CUSHIONS
ON THE BED

Just what is the point of these (answers on a postcard, please)? You go to bed at night. You throw all the cushions onto a chair. Next morning, you get up, you make the bed, you take the cushions from the chair and re-arrange them on top of the duvet. Why? Who the hell sees them? What is their function?

Do you really need this sort of clutter in your life? Ask yourself the above questions and if you can come up with sensible answers, fine, keep the damn things. But if you find yourself lost for a reasonable answer, send them to the charity shop immediately. Some sad professional housewife will be overjoyed to have them and you'll have gained an extra five minutes for lounging in the bath or applying an extra coat of polish to your toenails.

IRONING

Only do what you must!

I have a friend who irons her husband's boxer shorts! Can you believe it? I have another who irons the bedding. Silly girls!

Only iron what shows. Or pay someone else to do it. Our local dry cleaners have an ironing service. 50p per item. One shirt each for you and your partner for every day of the working week would cost £5. Worth it? I think so. What else can you buy for £5? Not a lot!

Only a maniac would iron bedding! I fold mine and store it in the airing cupboard. That's flat enough for me.

If your husband makes a fuss about little creases in his boxer shorts, I'd be very suspicious if I were you. Ask leading questions, he'll soon shut up - or iron his own.

If you are faced with a mountain of ironing you can't avoid, treat yourself to a video and a bottle of wine while you do it. And send your partner out to fetch a takeaway - you can't possibly cook as well* - there are limits!

*Or see 'cooking'.

COOKING

These days, a lot of people don't. They exist entirely on microwave meals and packet foods. Personally, I've got too much respect for my taste buds to go down that road - I'm also deeply suspicious of ingredients that sound like a chemistry set. So I do cook. But there's nothing to stop you taking some of the tedium out of it by buying ready-prepared vegetables, washed salad leaves, filleted fish, beautifully trimmed meat. Expensive? Not if you want quality and quantity.

And why should you have the monopoly on the joys of the kitchen? Men can cook really well if they're given the chance. So can your kids. The trick is not to fuss while they're doing it. Don't despair at the number of pans being used, the chaos, the general incompetence, the time it takes. Set the table, open the wine, pick up a book and relax. When the meal (eventually) appears, praise it, praise it, praise it. Here's a sample script to get you going:

Hmm, this is nice. I like the way you've given the steak that slightly singed taste. Very innovative.

Gosh, mushy sprouts. You clever thing!

Oh! Banana and sausage pizza! How unusual.

I do like the gravy - what an interesting texture. A smooth sauce is so bland, don't you think?

There's a line for every dish, I guarantee it. Whatever you do, never criticise.

POTS AND PANS

You couldn't be blamed here for being blinded by choice: coloured; patterned; floral; enamelled; non-stick; ceramic; with glass lids; with matching lids; stacking; straight-sided; rounded; plain; fancy; for gas hobs; for Agas; for electric hobs; cheap; expensive; middle of the road ... You can even buy pans to match your co-ordinated tablecloths, curtains and kitchen notice board - if you want to be truly pathetic, you'll go for the whole set, complete with matching apron, in which case you're probably a lost cause. But if you haven't gone down that route, don't waste time agonising. Buy the best stainless steel pans you can afford - burnt on dinners can be soaked off and, best of all, they happily go into the dish washer. You do have a dish washer don't you?

THE DISH WASHER

Every home should have one. It takes 5 minutes to load or empty (unless your husband does the loading, in which case he'll insist on washing everything before it goes in. His problem, not yours.) How much standing-at-the-sink time does that save? It's more hygienic, too - no more grubby tea towels spreading microbes all over the clean dishes. If you need an excuse to justify buying one, that should do for starters.

Some people (mainly husbands) will argue they don't have room for a dish-washer. Well, make room! I kicked my washing machine into the shed to accommodate mine. Think of it this way - which do you spend most time washing? Clothes or dishes? I rest my case.

Once you've bought this paragon of efficiency, you'll wonder how you ever managed without it. You'll be less bothered about dirtying pans and mixers and things, so you'll indulge in more creative cooking. Having prepared a nice dinner, you'll want to sit and linger over it, knowing the obedient servant in the kitchen is dealing with the pots. Your partner will be pleased as well, ecstatic to be enjoying the pleasure of your frazzle-free company.

Everybody happy. What an excellent investment.

KITCHEN KNICK-KNACKS

I don't know how I've done it, but I've managed all my life to do without a ceramic spoon rest. I have! I've also pottered quite happily in my kitchen without hanging silk ferns, potted plastic plants, special egg containers in the shape of a chicken or a wooden spoon receptacle disguised as a pig dressed up as a butcher.

Believe me, you can live without a spoon rest. If you're afraid to put it down on the work-top, an old saucer will do, or a tea plate, or a bit of scrunched tin-foil. (These spoons, whatever do they do to get so tired?)

Eggs can live in the box can't they? Less likely to get broken anyway - and did you know the best way to store an egg is pointy end up? Well, you do now. And the best way to keep their pointy ends up is to store them in the box.

I don't even want to discuss the introduction of silk ferns and plastic plants. Are you mad? You might just as well put up a sign saying 'Grease land here and give me extra grief.' The same goes for fridge magnets. One or two to anchor your shopping lists etc. - fine. But two hundred or so? What happens when you have a sudden rush of blood to the head and the urge to wipe down the fridge door?

KITCHEN GIMMICKS

You've only got to look through one of those catalogues that come through the door ... Fascinating reading it might be, but avoid the gimmicks you didn't realise you needed. The truth is, you don't! Unless you're really keen to clag up your kitchen storage space with inessentials, the following is a small list of items you really can do without:

- special dinky knives with 'pizza', 'cheese' or 'bread' stamped out of the blades - one good knife will do the lot;
- little gadgets that cut eggs or tomatoes into all manner of fancy shapes - you'll use them once;
- special egg-beating machines - a bowl and a fork or a whisk is all you require;
- grating gadgets - they never work properly and dismantling them for washing is more trouble than it's worth.
- glass chopping boards - eek! You can buy professional plastic ones for a about £1.50 which are unbreakable
- ditto fancy cheese and chopping boards which are not machine washable - stick with the plain plastic ones.

A housewife and her money are easily parted. Stick with what you need and forgo the gimmicks. The money you save will buy a meal out now and again. Which would you rather have? A kitchen full of gadgets or the occasional candlelit supper which somebody else has cooked? No contest!

BARBECUES

Love them or hate them, it's the one time a man can be guaranteed to don a silly pinny with tits on it, and actually produce something almost edible without complaining. I don't know why it should be so - maybe they like to pretend they're out in the wilds, roasting haunch of freshly-killed bear over a campfire - back to the days when men were men, women stayed home in the cave, and there was still an element of danger in providing the daily dinosaur. It doesn't matter why, make the most of it.

But don't be conned into providing bowls of salad and yards of garlic bread. Also avoid hovering in the kitchen with the cooker on stand-by in case of charcoal failure. Leave them to it.

Why not pop down to the pub for a few drinks while dinner is prepared? If you imbibe enough, you won't care if the sausages are raw and the burgers are burnt. Don't forget the yum-yum routine (see 'Cooking') to encourage a repeat performance.

Oh - and don't offer to clear away and wash up - far more flattering if you fall into a burger-induced snooze in front of the TV.

SANDWICHES

"What shall we have for lunch?"

"Don't go to any trouble, sweetheart, just make a few sandwiches."

Groan. No trouble? Sandwiches are a pain to make. Just because there isn't any cooking involved, it doesn't make it an easy job. By the time you've sliced, buttered, chopped eggs, washed lettuce, spread mustard, shredded chicken, drained the fish, grated cheese, peeled and sliced onions, assembled the ingredients neatly on the bread slices ... oh stop it, I've bored myself half to death just thinking about it.

The answer is the do-it-yourself sandwich.

Method: Lead the family into the kitchen.

Point out the bread bin.

Open the fridge and itemise all the goodies on the shelves.

When faced with blank looks, make a demo sandwich with flourish and verve.

Firmly state your intention of eating demo sandwich yourself. Leave the room.

They'll join you shortly. Whatever you do, don't make a fuss if your six year old is eating a cornflake, carrot and chocolate biscuit double-decker. Smile sweetly and tell them all how much you've enjoyed your 10 minutes of leisure. Perhaps they'll make your sandwich as well next time.

AN EVEN BETTER DO IT YOURSELF TEA FOR THE KIDS

I didn't invent this brilliant idea. Credit must go to Mrs Kennedy of 29 Hunt Street, Liverpool, circa 1950-something. Once a week, the Kennedy kids were each given a shilling (if you can't remember shillings, aren't you young? It's now worth 5p) and sent to the greengrocer. There was a competition to see who could buy the most pieces of fruit for their shilling and this, together with bread and margarine, was their tea. Voluntary vitamins! Come to think of it, if good old Mrs K was alive today, she could be writing this book. She was the first in our street to have a washing machine. While all the other mums were clucking about it not getting the clothes clean, she was saying she didn't care, just so long as they'd been swirled through soapy water. What a star! In the time saved not labouring over the wash tub, she played the piano, sang beautifully, and could sometimes be prevailed upon to demonstrate an Irish jig. Thank God she had the sense to put her time to good use.

DINNER PARTIES: Food

There's nothing nicer than sharing a meal with friends. If you're hosting that meal, there's the added bonus that you don't need to go home afterwards. You can stagger up to bed and collapse in a heap. You can even collapse on the floor if you want to. Nobody need know.

On the other hand, there's nothing worse than inviting people to dinner and spending a whole week agonising, worrying and preparing. No need. Honestly.

Ask yourself these questions:

Are they coming to criticise my food? Or are they coming to enjoy my company?

If the answer to the first question is 'yes', you need to ask yourself why you want these people in your house. Surely life's too short to be spending time in the company of people you don't really like. Lot's of people do it. Are you one of them?

Having got that out of the way, and undesirable visitors crossed off your list, you can relax about entertaining people you really like. They won't care if the meal is not cordon bleu - they really won't. Cottage pie and beans in convivial company, served by a relaxed and smiling hostess, is vastly superior to beuf en croute with a side order of nervous breakdown

DINNER PARTIES: Housework

Should you do a major spring-clean in preparation for your guests? Well, if it's going to stress you out and make you wish you'd never asked them: NO! Nobody cares. And if they do they're not your friends, why would you want to entertain them? Really, life can be so simple if you don't allow it to be difficult.

If you are really uneasy about the dust or the shabbiness of your wallpaper, switch off the main lights and dine by candlelight. This has the added advantage of concealing your wrinkles and will put everybody in a mellow mood.

Whatever you do - leave the washing up till the guests have gone. Honestly, there's nothing worse than a frazzled hostess faffing about with much clattering and table-clearing. It's also irritating, ill-mannered, makes the guests feel guilty and can lead to a martyred expression and a migraine attack. Retire to the lounge with brandy and coffee and forget about the dishes. If you don't have a lounge or prefer to stay at the table, just clear away the worst of the clutter and stack it in the sink. Stay with your guest, scintillate and enjoy.

And remember - when you go to their homes for dinner, you can sit back with a clear conscience and not insult them by offering to do their washing up.

DINNER PARTIES: Attending

If you've followed the advice of the previous two chapters, the chances are you've had some lovely times with your guests. Thus encouraged, and having been served simple food in a not too tidy house by a hostess who didn't give a damn about appearances, your friends will probably be tempted to follow suit. So the chances are you'll be invited to dine out much more often than if you'd turned your own dinner party into the sort of production number nobody could hope to emulate.

The perfect guest doesn't offer to help with the washing up. The perfect guest turns up with a couple of bottles of nice wine and maybe some flowers. The perfect guest enjoys herself (but not to the extent where she passes out under the table). The perfect guest knows when to go home. If your hostess appears in her dressing gown with a toothbrush in her hand, you've out-stayed your welcome.

CLEANING THE TOILET

This has to be the worst job on the domestic front and nobody else ever seems to notice it needs doing. But if you have a partner who's a creature of habit and spends half an hour in there every morning with the paper, you can turn this to your advantage. You know the signs. Watch him carefully and, just as he's about to retreat to his early morning haven, nip in there before him and squirt bathroom mousse all over the seat, the lid, the cistern, as well as a generous helping in the bowl. What can he do? His bowels are sending messages which can't be ignored. He has no choice but to clean up his throne before he can ascend it.

This may well lead to an Exchange of Words - but you will have made your point.

THE BATHROOM

If there's anybody in the house entitled to hog the bathroom, it's you. It probably has a lock on the door - use it. An hour of solitude and sanctuary. Bliss.

Give everyone fair warning before you enter - especially if the only loo is in the same room. Make it perfectly clear that you're not going to leap out of the bath to let anybody in for a wee.

Keep your bathroom simple and clutter-free. You don't want to waste precious time clearing up other people's junk when you can be relaxing in a warm aroma-therapy bath with a good book and something nice to drink. If you find odd socks, slippers or discarded newspapers on the floor, bin them. No messing. Straight into the bin with them. The same goes for after-shave, perfume, make-up, tweezers, spot-cream, fake tan and disposable razors not put away where they belong. It takes long enough to clean the sink and the bath (we've already dealt with the toilet) without having to shift a ton of junk before you start.

Partners and children should be strongly encouraged to join a gym or a sports club and to swim regularly - not only will it keep them fit, healthy and out of your hair, they'll shower before they come home!

ORNAMENTS

We're back to the dust issue here. OK, it's a bleak sort of home that doesn't have a bit of something or other dotted about for decoration - but if you must go in for knick-knacks, stick to a few large ones as opposed to a lot of small ones. Less to shift about in the dusting department. Whatever you do, don't start a collection of anything. The word only has to get out that you're partial to pigs, hippos, owls, ducks, crinoline ladies or fancy teapots and you'll be inundated with the damn things every Christmas and birthday when all you really wanted was a nice box of chocolates or a bottle of bubble bath.

On second thoughts, put the word about that you're starting a collection of fine wine, unusual whisky, speciality gin … I leave it to your imagination.

Happy Birthday to me, indeed!

PLASTIC FRUIT

Do me a favour! You haven't, have you? How embarrassing. Well quick, bung it straight into the bin under cover of darkness - I won't tell a soul. China fruit is almost as bad, but has the advantage of being machine-washable (our hero the dishwasher again) without melting. But think on, artificial fruit, be it plastic or ceramic, is only another ornament. I don't think it's even fashionable these days - but the real thing is. The real thing is beautiful, decorative and edible. It's also full of vitamins and fibre. So why would you want to give house-room to the artificial sort? Leave it where it belongs, in shop-window displays and wine bars.

CANDLES

Candles are great. They can be decorative, romantic, soothing, sensual. If you've had a bad day, there's nothing nicer than candlelight, your favourite music and a little drink of something or other. Candlelight flatters the complexion and softens the contours of clutter.

They make super gifts and the best ones I've found recently come in their own little glass. Burn the candle, scrape out the left-over wax, shove the glass through our friend the dishwasher and there you have a perfect receptacle for gin and tonic or single malt. Just the job.

Bear in mind though, if you don't burn them, they become 'ornaments' and gather dust like it's going out of fashion. And why wouldn't you? Some people never do, do they? I wonder why? I can't resist setting fire to the little buggers.

So how many virgin candles do you have taking up valuable shelf space? Go on - apply a match to a wick or two, dim the lights - and stand by for a mood change for the better.

SHOPPING

We're talking about food shopping here. Essential-supplies-shopping. Shopping that involves bread, baked beans, bog roll, bleach, bananas and boredom.

What you must never do is lunch-time shopping. Your lunch hour is for lunch. If you must use part of it for shopping, make sure it's nice shopping - shoes, books, pressies, flowers, more shoes. Do you ever see a man staggering back to the office with supermarket carrier bags, so low on blood sugar he has to snack on a Mars Bar before he can begin work? Not bloody likely! The only staggering he'll be doing is due to an excess of lunchtime alcohol. No, ladies, it's your duty to give yourself time off mid-day. If the cupboard is bare, tough titty, you'll just have to eat out that night. I'm not very good at shopping, I bring home mangoes instead of light bulbs, I forget the toothpaste, and I'm inclined to hyperventilate if the checkout queue is more than three people long. So my partner shops, I cook what he brings home and we're all happy.

The moral of this is that we all should stick to what we enjoy. If neither of you can manage the dreaded weekly shop, there's always home delivery. Whatever you do, if you both hate shopping, don't do it together - therein lies the rocky road to disharmony!

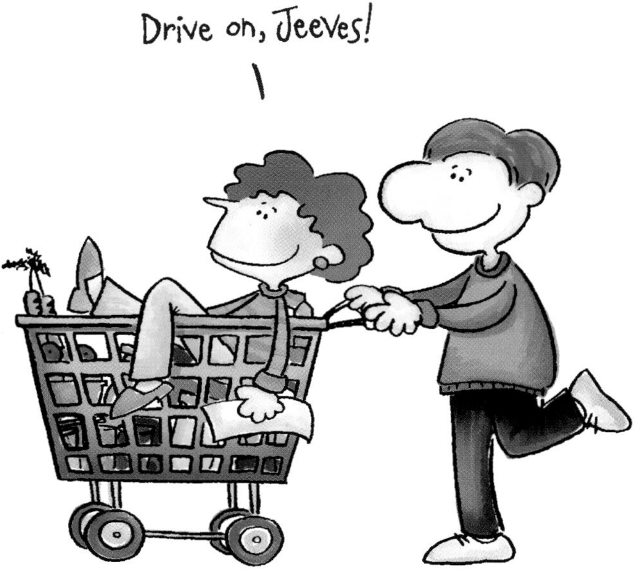
Drive on, Jeeves!

TODDLERS AND TIDINESS

Short of locking the little darlings in a cupboard with their toys, it'll never happen, so don't waste energy fretting about it. Instead, adopt the attitude that children should be enjoyed - if they're not to be enjoyed, why go to the trouble of having them in the first place? See playing with your little ones as a perfect excuse for not doing more tedious things. What would you rather be doing - building a Lego space station or tidying the airing cupboard? Washing down paintwork or feeding ducks in the park? No contest really, is there? And if you keep them busy and amused right through the day, chances are they'll go to bed without a quibble - they'll be glad to escape from your manic programme of activities!

KIDS AT SCHOOL

OK - an extra five shirts in the ironing basket for every child at school. You could always form a committee and lobby for sweatshirts as part of the uniform ...

There'll be lunch boxes and homework, pleas to stay up late because 'everybody else does' and, quite probably, your older offspring turning up with half a dozen friends, looking for something to eat. This is where your DIY sandwich training comes into its own. Ask them to make one for you while they're about it.

It's well worth going to the trouble of encouraging your young ones to have their friends to stay. It's not a lot more trouble and, with a bit of luck, the parents of the friends will reciprocate. Just think - an empty house, no interruptions ... say no more, crack open a bottle and set light to some of those candles.

TEENAGERS

I know, they hardly bear thinking about, but we've all been through this stage so I suppose we should be sympathetic. The main thing to remember is that they're like spiders - more afraid of you than you are of them.

Never forget that they're suffering from raging hormones, so it's not going to be a lot of use if you bombard them with the nagging artillery. You're supposed to be the mature one. Even when you feel like having hysterics and beating them about the head with their own smelly socks, you have to be cool.

Whatever you do, don't interfere with their rooms! (I can't imagine why anybody would want to, they're always disgusting!) If they leave their stuff on the stairs or in the middle of the kitchen or any other place where it's likely to cause offence or inconvenience, merely throw it through their bedroom doorway. Where it lands is not your problem.

They are, by this stage, old enough to deal with their own laundry. Don't be a mug. If they don't have clean jeans or shirts, it's not your responsibility. Do not weaken. Do not give in to cries of anguish when they can't find an uncreased shirt for Saturday night. If they don't know how to use an iron by this stage, you have only yourself to blame.

CONCLUSION

So what does it all boil down to? An unhappy housewife is a hateful hag. She's the victim of the myth that you have to do all this stuff. You don't. If you live alone, I don't expect you have any problem, because you're at liberty to please yourself. The pressure comes from family living. If you share your home with others, spread the load. Delegate. But above all, don't let yourself get into a pooh about stuff that doesn't really matter. If your family is nourished, reasonably clean most of the time, harmonious and happy, what more do you want? What more could any sane person possibly want?